Inspirational Poetry

To Prick Your Heart, Convict Your Soul & Renew Your Mind

Poems Written by

Muletta Hayes

Cover Designed by Emanuel Antunes

ISBN: 978-1-7342540-2-0

R.D. Talley Books Publishing
P.O. Box 45
Plainsboro, New Jersey 08536
www.rdtalleybooks.com

Dedications

First and foremost, I would like to thank God, who is the head of my life for giving me this gift. It is because of Him that I am.

In memory of my mother, Mrs. Hattie Bernice King. Missing you so much and I know you are smiling down on me.

In memory of my Aunt Hilda Smith, who raised me to become the woman I am today. She always told me, "If Sally can do it, so can you." She was right, as usual. My 2nd Mom.

To my Aunt Thelma Smith, who was always there for me. I consider myself to be one of hers.

And finally,

To my husband James and my children; Maliah, Ja She' and James III and all of my grandchildren.

I love you all! You are my life!

Contents

A Witness or A Spectator

A witness can give or serve evidence of
one whom can testify to
A spectator is one who watches at a show
game, event or preview

It's time to get off the sideline
thinking church is just a show
Or just sitting in your seats
blankly like you don't even know

Christianity is not a spectator sport
where you can sit and watch in the stands
It's time to make a joyful noise
unto the Lord, all Ye lands

We're not here to be an onlooker
we are doers of our savior Jesus Christ
who paid our debt of sin
with the ultimate sacrifice

Once you become a witness
things will never be the same
From inside to out you will rejoice
and his goodness you will acclaim

Why be a spectator when you can be a witness?
To testify of all his glory
share the gospel to everyone
to share Jesus' story

Jesus loved you enough to sacrifice
Now what will you do to repay?
Will you be a witness or just a spectator?
Your choice begins today.

Awake

Some people are still asleep
and their walk of life is in vain
Their hearts yearn for so much more
and it suffers greatly in pain

Their days to them seem just
because they go to their place of work and back
Not realizing they have a purpose
and peace and joy they lack

You would not drive a car sleepy
or fall asleep on your job
But when it comes to you being spiritual awake
your sleeping soul…you rob

People who are asleep are inactive
occupied with daily pleasure or wealth
Showing little concern to their spiritual needs
weakening their spiritual health

In order to inherit the Kingdom of God
one must be born again
An awakening in their spirit
putting away a life full of sin

Jesus told his disciples
to watch while he pray
But they did not listen to him and fell asleep
as we do to him today

He also said weeping may endure for a night
but joy come in the morn
Morning does not just mean the AM
but when you awake from your storm

It's time to wake up
get busy doing God's will
Avoid works belonging to the darkness
and sometimes being still

Be aware of the danger of spiritual slumber
try new ways to preach
Remember the importance of your ministry
and the goals we must reach

It's time to watch as well as pray
You can't wait for the earth to shake
Spread the Word of God
to do so …. You must be AWAKE

Are You In?

There's a spiritual warfare going on
that some know nothing about
A fight for your mind and your soul
either you are in or you are out.

There is no in-between
that's why God needs to abide within
To cover, protect, and keep you
so with Him you will win

You have an enemy, understand that
it's not fair or fun, but a fact
He's manipulative, cunning and wants your soul
and from God, he'll do everything to distract

He's going to try to get under your skin
ruin you, kill you, keep you from trying to serve
Try to pull you away from God
all the things you don't deserve

Try to deter you from your destiny
prolonging your weeping night
But now is the time you must gird up
make up your mind, the devil you will fight

Ready to take him on
with the whole armor from head to feet
Standing firm like an old oak tree
not backing down, nor will you retreat

God's word is an indispensable weapon
prayer is essential, pray to continue in His will
So when it's all over and the dust clear up
you will be on your feet still

As soon as you have a made-up mind
God will intervene, a fight guaranteed a win
My question for you today is
Are you out…or are you in??

Are You Hungry?

"Blessed are those who hunger and thirst for righteousness, for they shall be filled." -Matthew 5:6, NIV

To hunger is to have a need
to crave, or have a desire
And if the hunger abides in you
then something should transpire

If you're hungry for God's Word
you'll begin to use it for fuel
To fill you up from day to day
eating in bible study and feasting in Sunday School

For He is the bread of life.
if you come you shall not hunger; if you believe,
you shall not thirst…
Blessed is the man who trusts in Him
and always puts him first

A hungry person shows up expecting
sitting at the table waiting to be fed
Preparing their hearts and their minds
to receive their daily bread

With each taste, which fulfills
even more sweeter than before
But you're still hungry...really hungry
wanting even more

The more you eat...the more you want
the more you begin to grow
Trusting...believing....being steadfast
your faith will begin to flow

It's time to have forbearance
self-control ...no time to play
Get in deep in God's Word with understanding
Are you hungry today?

Are You Ready For A Change?

Are you ready to be changed
transmuted, transformed?...
A complete spiritual overhaul
in God's way conformed?

Are you in the midst of a spiritual outage
no power, no zest, or no zeal?
Then a change is what you need
to start, get on the potter's wheel

No one said it will be easy
to be on the potter's wheel
To be shaped and to be molded
and sometimes just having to be still

It's time to stir up the flames in your life
and create in you a fire,
Combust and ignited for God
a change, a transformation…. a desire

Some days you will feel crushed
and some, you may be in the dark
You'll feel sometimes pressed
but that's just God leaving his mark

Remember diamonds are formed under pressure
olives are pressed to release oil
Grapes must be crushed to make wine
and seeds grow in the darkness beneath the soil

The pain, tribulations, and transformation
is all worth the cost
To be created into something new
for those of us who are lost

He is here waiting patiently
for you to hand your life to rearrange
Come to Him, give Him all of you
and get ready for your change

(to come in and sup with you
but are you ready for a change?)

A Press In Your Spirit

Press is to move or cause to move into a position
with something by exerting continuous physical force
To clasp, ram, wedge or thrust
pushing your way to the source

The woman with the issue of blood
had enough faith to press her way through
She knew who Jesus was
and all that He could do

For she said to herself
"If only I may touch His garment I should be made well"
She believed that Jesus could heal her
and by her faith, He could tell

She had a press in her spirit
a determination, a robust
Focused, she made her way through the crowd
for In Jesus, she did trust

You must be like the woman
who was hanging from a limb
Who pressed her way to Jesus
just to touch His hem

Not only did she press
but she had faith and she was bold
And because of that
her faith made her whole

Now there is no need to fight a crowd
you can reach Him just the same
Any time, day or night, all you have to do
is call on Jesus' name

For He is the key
in Him you can find rest
He will heal, deliver and set you free
just in your spirit, find a press

Are You Ready For Your New Thing?

"A new heart also will I give you, and a new spirit will I put within you: and I will take away the stony heart out of your flesh, and I will give an heart of flesh." – Ezekiel 36:26, KJV

"Behold, I will do a new thing; now it shall spring forth; shall ye not know it? I will even make a way in the wilderness, and rivers in the desert." – Isaiah 43:19, KJV

Are you ready for your new thing?
Are you ready for your start?
Do you want to be made anew?
And have created in you a clean heart?

You should not want to be restored
returned to a former condition, place or position,
Repaired… renovated…as if to return
to its original condition

But you should desire to be new
made, introduced, fresh, not existing before
Allowing God to use you
as his love for you outpour

He found you in the cluster
as in Isaiah, he found the new wine
He did not destroy, for there was a blessing
and a blessing in you, his own design

Allow your heart to open
and your soul to soar
Once you're on the potter's wheel
you won't be as you were before

As you remember the oneness
and his spirit dwells within
That will be the truth of your essence
and a new you will begin

God does not want to repair or renovate
but a new you he wants to bring
Enter your life, cleaning your heart, purifying your soul
The question is…are you ready for your new thing?

Beautifully Broken

To be broken is to be fractured
damaged, giving up hope, to be in despair
To feel alone, sometimes unworthy
shattered, defeated, believing no one really care

But if we would just trust Him
and hand God the pieces of our mess
He would blow on it, heal it, use us
and through it, we would be blessed

For He uses broken things beautifully
to create in it anew
And through your brokenness
he wants to create anew in you

Through broken clouds, we get rain
which waters the grass so it will grow
And a broken white light splits into seven colors
to give as a beautiful rainbow

When soil is broken it sets a field
broken crops yield seeds in strife
The broken seeds leads to a plant
and gives it a new life

God uses all our broken pieces
to make something beautiful, on Him, patiently wait
For through you, in you He wants to use you
and utilize you for something great

For everything you thought you lost, you will gain
without the dark, you wouldn't see a star
This is just a pause in your sentence
Beautifully Broken is only what you are.

Do You Know How Big Your God Is?

Do you know how big your God Is?
Do you really understand??
What it means as Alpha and Omega?
He is no ordinary man!

Do you know all that he can do
in the blink of an eye, a drop of a hat?
He can turn a situation around
or take someone home just like that

He created this world
with his Holy hands
He divided the water and dirt
and scooped up the sands

He formed the mountains and shaped the trees
and set the atmosphere
before he even began
to place his precious children here

He knows you distinctively
before you were even a thought
He knew every mistake you would make
every battle you would have fought

He formed you in his womb
before your mother was blessed
He knew she would assist him
and then he gave you breath

You were created for a purpose
within your everyday living
And that's to worship him, the father
the rest is just a giving

This powerful God loves you
but sometimes one tends to put him on a shelf
He created you for his purpose
for only himself

He wants his children to have the best
he sent his only son to die for you
Now if Our God would do that
what more for you he won't do??

Stop telling God how big your problem is
he knows for you are his
It's not big nor a surprise to him
tell your problem how big your God is.

He's Working It Out For You

Storms may come our way
and if it's not one thing, it's another
Trying to break you down
and in your spirit stir

You try to bear it down
holding on to all that abides in you
Knowing, trusting and believing
you'll soon see your breakthrough

God has a plan
nothing catches him by surprise
But we must remember to stay focused
with the prize within our eyes

We were set aside for his purpose
he never said our days would be trial free
Taking one day at a time
with his grace and his mercy

I know things seem disarray right now
and how long must be your days
But God knows all about it
and trouble don't last always

Gods timing is not our timing
be still and know he'll give you rest
Your creator, your father
for you, he knows what's best.

He loves you, he has not forgotten
trust he will see you through
No matter what it looks like
He's working it out for you.

In The Midst Of Your Storm

If you find yourself in a storm
because you failed to listen or launched out thereon
The storm is lasting too long
don't give up but keep the faith and hold on

Just like Paul and his crew
who had made it to the shore
Just as God had promised
in his Holy Word before

Even in the midst of a storm
the Lord has the last say
The author and finisher of our faith
no need to be frightened or dismay

Know that your soul is anchored
to the one that hung, bled and died
And through his generous act of love
our debts of sin were satisfied

He promised never to leave or forsake us
he is with us everywhere we go
Especially in the storms of our lives
allowing in us, his love for us to overflow

He will make a way out of no way
he will see you through
He will be right there
to lead and guide you

"And behold I am with you
until the end of age"
That even means
when the storm begins to rage

Just keep on praying, believing and trusting
in His will, be conform
But whatever you may do
don't give up in your storm

Is Your All On The Altar?

Is your all on the altar?
Did you surrender everything?
Your heart, mind, spirit, body and soul
Did you lay it before the King?

In order for him to fix it
and make sure everything is on track,
You must leave it with him
and not pick it up and take it back

Is your all on the altar?
Did you release and submit?
Your wants, your fears, your desires
your all…nothing do you omit

He can use anyone
any time, any day or place
He can change and rearrange
he can fill a void or an empty space

Is your all on the altar?
Are you ready to be blessed?
Rise up and receive your deliverance
and a release from your mess

There's no fear or shame
he'll catch you when you fall
Just meet him at the altar
cast your cares and give him your all.

It's Time To Wake Up

It's time to awake out of your sleep
it's time to seek his face
Seek him while he can be found
and in his love, embrace

It's time to become aware
and fully conscience of his word
Unconscious and unaware, we will miss him
and that's clearly unheard

There's a war within all of us
the war between spirit and flesh
The flesh that's not led by God
and the spirit everyday refresh

The flesh says be comfortable, you have time
The spirit says don't get slack,
Always be ready and on guard
because you never know when I'll be back

The flesh says to rest
the spirit says stay up with me and fight
The flesh loves confusion
the spirit wants to make it right

It's really time to wake up saints
time to do it today
Abide yourself in God's Word
and watch as well as pray.

Just Be Brave

You're made in God's image
appointed from the womb
A life to be filled with joy and peace
and not darkness, depression or gloom
But, unfortunately there's a spirit
which stops our growing and persevere
It puts our blessings literally on hold
it's called the spirit of fear
Fear will take away your vision
it will cause you to be in distress
Make you think all kinds of thoughts
and cause a whole lot of confusion and mess
The spirit of fear will hover over you
and wait for negativity to escape your lips
That's when it gets a little stronger
and tightens its ugly grip
But if you just focus on God
put him first in all you do
When you see God first
then you will be able to see yourself too
When you can stand in God
you don't have to be afraid
For he'll give you power, love and a sound mind
and his love is everlasting, it will never fade
Trust and believe God
for greatness in your life to come
Have faith and praise him in advance
for he is awesome
It's time to bind this spirit
stop running to our safety cave
Replace fear with faith
and Just Be Brave

Let Go Of The Knob

Some of you are holding doors
and delaying your blessing
Trying to control what's not in your control
and continuously messing

Your hand is on the door handle
your foot holding the door ajar
Not realizing that without God
you won't get very far

God is willing and able
to do exceedingly beyond and above
He already showers you with his blessings
and comforts you with his wondrous love

He wants to create in you a new
and abide in you within
Be a part of your everyday life
the brokenness…he will mend

He loves you unconditionally
like no one ever before
Behold he stands knocking
just open up your heart's door

He will make ways out of no way
amaze you and astound
Let you know that he is near
his existence is profound

He will open doors you thought were locked
and close them as needed for you
But you are blocking the door
holding the handle and peeping through

He wants to be your all in all
wipe your tears if and when you sob
The first step is up to you
simply…let go of the knob

Let Him In

You feel the tugging at your heart
you hear the knocking at the door
You're experiencing some spiritual things
like you've never experienced before

Jesus wants to sup with you
he wants in you to abide
Create in you something new
and in your heart, reside

He doesn't want you lukewarm
but hot or cold you must choose
He wants to be the head of your life
you've received several clues

He sees the tears that you cry
he hears your every moan
He promised never to leave you
so you will never be alone

But there seems to be an issue
as your heart begins to yearn
The door to your heart is closed
and only by you can the knob be turned

It's time to open the door
to change all of you within
Jesus is the only one who can
if you just let him in.

Meet God By The Pool

It's time to seek your healing
time to press pass the pain
It's time to stop blaming others
it's time to weather some rain

You have to prepare for what you're expecting
know and trust in God's Word
Praying without ceasing
and believing your prayers are heard

Stop waiting on yourself
position yourself in the right place
So God can meet you there
and your blessing you will embrace

What are you waiting on
when he's asking will you be healed today
Move to your expectancy
you never know when he's heading your way

Un-crowd your life with extras
and begin to focus on his glory
Allow praise and worship to take over
and let your life tell the story

First and most important
in order for your fire to get fuel
You must acknowledge that you need him
and then meet him by the pool

More Than Enough

When times get hard
and your road seems rough
Just trust in God
he's more than enough

Trust and believe
he will see you through
Lead and guide you
and take care of you

How big is your faith?
The size of a mustard seed?
Don't you know he loves you
and will supply all your needs?

When my way gets weary
I'm knee deep and it gets tough
I keep my focus on him
for he is more than enough

What we see is not what he sees
he's fixing all of your stuff
For his plan, his purpose, his will
because he is more than enough.

Persistent Prayer

Persistent means to continue firmly
in spite of difficulty or opposition
To be tenacious, determined, untiring and patient
basically…on a mission

Persistent prayer never hesitates or grow weary
never discouraged or yield to fear
But is lifted-up and sustained by hope
knows no despair and a faith that persevere

Persistent prayer has patience to wait
and strength to continue too
It never quits, it refuses to give up
until it reaches a breakthrough

Are you just reciting words in vain?
Or muttering the same ole line…unfree?
Or are you trying to reach the heavens
and let God hear your plea?

Persistent prayer brings about hope and faith to flourish
and you trust as well as believed
Praying without ceasing or tiring…staying on your knees
until your answer is received

So if you desire for God to hear from you
you're troubled and in despair
Just come to him diligently, determined, with a made-up mind
with your persistent prayer

Please Remember Me

Just like the thief upon the cross
who longed to be set free
I pray to you my Lord and Savior
please remember me

When the saints are called up
and the rapture starts to be
I beg of you my Alpha and Omega
please remember me

When I don't know how to pray
and the clouds block what I see
Please guide my every footstep
and please remember me

If I stumble, I pray I won't fall
or if I run and flee
Please my God have mercy on my soul
and please remember me

Take my hand and lead me Lord
I'm on my bending knee
Begging and pleading to you
to please remember me

Renew Your Mind

"And be not conformed to this world: but be ye transformed by the renewing of your mind, that ye may prove what is that good, and acceptable, and perfect, will of God." – Romans 12:2, KJV

In order to be totally free
you must first renew your mind
Your body can come out of the cursed place
but your mind needs to be refined

The Israelites were free
but their mentality was still as a slave
Wandering forty years through the wilderness
and it led some to an early grave

God is trying to bring you out of things
that your mind wants to keep you in
But your mind needs to be renewed by God's Word
and let his spirit abide within

If there is no change in your thinking
you may follow the path like the wife of Lot
Who was free but because of her mentality
believed that she was not

These shows and music are meant to change your mindset
tighten the shackles and chains that bond you
To draw you further from the Will of God
and accept the things that God said to not do

These things bring people into a cursed state
back in bondage, cause you to digress
It's time to wake up and renew your mind
and get free of all that mess!

The Dash In Between

There will be two dates on your tombstone
but what will it mean??
All that is really going to matter
is the dash in between

The dash represents
our life here on earth
All the work that we did
and what it was worth

Not what title we held
or riches and such
But how did we minister
and the lives that we touched

We can make the meaning of our dash
mean so much more
If we love like Jesus loves us
and the holy spirit, we don't ignore

Try to spread God's Word
and every day do a good deed
Helping our fellow man
filling where there is a need

The most important part
of our days we are living
Is reaching out to others
our hearts and our giving

So when your family and friends read
your life through their tears
Your dash will remind them
all you've done through the years

There will be two dates on your tombstone
but what will it mean??
It's really up to you
how you fill the dash in between

There Is No God Like Him

There are many gods and lords
but for us, there is only one
And no one is like him
one to compare…no there's none

There is no one like God so we bow
to lower ourselves, we bend our knee
To be humble we bow our heads
for we know who set us free

We surrender as we raise our hands
we close our eyes to meditate
We lift our voice because we know where he is
the one who determines our fate

There is no other God so we acknowledge his promise
a mouth that promise, and all is kept
a hand that delivers and eyes that saw
who saved a world in debt

There is no one like God so we acknowledge his vastness
how great is our God, so immense
Heaven is his home, the earth is merely his footstool
but his love for us that's in it…is intense

He shows us every day how much he cares
he loved us so much he sent his son
And our obedience to God shows that we believe
like him…there is no other one

He is the one and only true living God
independent and shines a light when its dim
In heaven in absolute control
there is no one like him

Wait

One of the hardest things a person can do
during their lifetime is wait
Waiting requires patience, pain without complaint
bearing of provocation, suppressing the irritate

Waiting on God is just as hard
but if you don't faint, you will reap in your due season
He makes you wait for what he has for you
him and him alone knows the reason

Most people have a microwave mentality
and they get frustrated and want to quit,
But God won't hand you anything
without his fingerprint on it

God is working in your waiting…he sees and hears
nothing passes by his eye
Not only did Jesus come to save us
but He, himself, had to wait to die

Sometimes something is happening when nothing is happening
a change is taking place
Take heed to what you can not see
and know you're in God's loving embrace

Even during the silence, God is working
you wait…not for punishment but because He cares
Now is the time to look up and listen
trusting in the midst that He is there

No place is too dark and no wall is too thick
for God's grace to penetrate in a powerful and life-affirming way
He is in control…don't mind the wait
He's a constant comfort night and day

I will trust you, Oh Lord
during my wait, I will seek you all the more
Because your grace is sufficient enough for me
each day passing, more and more

I stretch my hand to you Father
Alpha and Omega…my redeemer, your holy name I'll elevate
Give me strength, bless my soul
as I patiently…on you…wait

Whose Hands Are You In?

In my hand a baseball bat is worth ten dollars
In Jackie Robinson's hand its worth millions
In my hand a basketball is worth twenty dollars
In Michael Jordan's hand its worth billions

A slingshot in my hands is useless
but a slingshot in David's hand, a giant he did slay
Two fish and five loaves of bread in my hand is a sandwich
but two fish and five loaves of bread in Jesus' hands fed a
multitude one day

In my hands, a nail will build something temporary
In Jesus' hands, a nail is worth your salvation
Who unselfishly sacrificed His life
to save all of God's creation

It matters whose hands you are in
because it determines your worth
Placed in His hands, he hung, bled and died
because you are his salt of the earth

He knew from the very beginning
that some may never love him in return
But still fulfilled his purpose with true love
he hoped they would soon learn

Once placed in his hands
none can be plucked out
He is yours, you are his
in your heart, there will be no doubt

He loves you unconditionally
he knew you before you were created
He watched as you grew
and on you, he patiently waited

For you to heartedly seek him
for He is right by your side
All the while you did not know
he was there to be your guide

For you in man's hands
Is not worth as much you see
But you in Gods hands
Is worth Life and Love Eternally

So my question for you today
as your life unfolds till the end
To love, to keep, to protect you…
Whose hands are you in?

You Are Not Forgotten

"See, I have engraved you on the palms of my hand; your walls are ever before me." – Isaiah 49:16, NIV

Sometimes you may feel lost
and some peace is what you search
You can't seem to find it anywhere
not even in the church

You feel weighed down
depression seems to take its toll
Your world seems to be falling apart
and spinning out of control

You try to humble yourself and pray
but wonder does God hear your cry
You get discouraged to the point
you say…why even try??

But I'm here to let you know
your life is for God's purpose and plan
He has not forgotten you
for you are engraved into his hand

He promised never to leave nor forsake you
to be there when you call
In hard times he will carry you
he will not let you fall

Tests come to make you strong
to build your faith and your trust
He wants you to shine like gold
not for you to wither or rust

Trials and tribulations
can be used to distract you
From what God desires for your life
and all he has for you to do

Do not get discouraged
trust and lean as you stand
Knowing that God is always with you
for you are embedded in his hand

You Met Him, But Do You Know Him?

Some people don't believe in God
because they don't know who He is
For if they knew the God I know
they would desire to be one of his

He is the Alpha and the Omega
When you're hanging on a limb
He's a fortress in the time of distress
and protects those who seek refuge in him

He is Jehovah Jirah, my provider
to see that every need is met
He's Jehovah Rapha, my healer
there is no need to worry or fret

Jehovah Nissi, my banner of victory
willing to warfare just for me
Jehovah Shalom who brings me peace
and because of him, I'm free

You have to get to know him for yourself
and through his word is the best way
He IS the word and all you'll need
feed on his word and pray

God wants to build a trust with you
and with you he wants to sup
He wants to abide in you and you in him
and overflow your cup

So you met him, but do you know him
and in your heart there is no doubt
Because once you get to know him
with HIM…you won't want to live without.

Your Condition Is Not Your Conclusion

All of us have a condition
whether it's favorable or not to us
But your condition is not your conclusion
if in God, we put your trust

God can change your condition
if you have faith, trust and believe
Fear not and faint not
and to his unchanging hand, you cleave

Conditioner...the hair care product
for a moment let's compare
It's used directly after washing
and changes the texture and appearance of the hair

Just like that conditioner
your condition will ultimately change you
Because after you're washed by the blood of the lamb
there will be things you may go through

But through understanding and prayer
then on your conclusion, you await
Knowing God will work it out
the author and finisher of our faith

God has declared you from the beginning
working on your conclusion from the start
Because you belong to him and him only
carrying a piece of his heart

Let the condition form and have peace
knowing your conclusion will soon unfold
Trust, have faith and know
that God is always in control

He's always on time
trouble don't always last
Look your eyes toward the hills
and know that this too shall pass

It's Worth The Cost

Connecting to your ministry or calling
is a great responsibility
No one knows your story or the price
the glory is all people see

Your calling sometimes won't be easy
you, it's going to crush and cost
But losing everything is well worth the price
saving the lives which are lost

If your calling is to mend the broken hearted
you're going to wrestle with broken heartedness
If your call is to prophesy
your mouth, you must learn to suppress

If you are called to lay hands
spiritual viruses will have to be lifted
If you're called to preach and teach the gospel
the wisdom that anoints your message will be sifted

If you are called to empower it will be attacked
your successes will be hard fought
But do not allow it to sway you
do not entertain any negative thought

In order for your mantle to be authentic, humble and with power
your calling will come with thorns and sifting
Remember what God has placed inside you
for in you, it will be uplifting

Your calling won't be easy because your assignment is not
for your oil is far from cheap
God will never ask you to give up more than he will give back
and through it all, you, He will keep

Trust his plans and his promise through the adversities
although to and from, you may be tossed
God's word sustains, he'll never desert you
and it will all be worth the cost

Are You A Squeezer Or A Pleaser?

Are you a squeezer or a pleaser?
This is the question for today
Do you take the time to get to know God
or are you even too busy to pray?

To answer this question
one must first be honest with self
Is God a major part of your day
or is he placed upon a shelf?

How you use each moment is a choice
He's either in the moment or pushed aside
You can't just squeeze him into your life
he has to dwell within you and abide

Many people try to make practicing
the presence of God into a part-time job
But God must be present in all moments
what is not just, it's yourself that you rob

Quality time is more important to God
than the quantity of such
He wants you to know him deeply
he loves you just that much

There's no limit to how good life can be
when God is first, he's pleased
Be full-time, praise him everyday
and your time with him won't be squeezed

Try to be more of a pleaser
It's the time, not the amount
For God can't be squeezed into your life
He only can be squeezed out

Why Are You Afraid?

Why are you going through life
with gloom, trembling, uncertain & unclear
When God has given you power, love, self-discipline
but NOT the spirit of fear

He is with you every season of your life
to protect you, correct you and reform
To guide you and to cover you
even in the midst of your storm

He will never leave you or forsake you
by your side, your victory, He will win it
Never out...He is always in the midst
when you call, He will be in it

He didn't keep Daniel from the lion's den
he met him there and took him higher
Didn't keep Shadrach, Meshach and Abednego from the furnace
but met them there...in the fire

Didn't keep Joseph from being a slave
but gave him favor so well
And when Joseph went to prison
he met him in the jail cell

God will meet you in your circumstance
there's no need to be dismayed
He will never leave you nor forsake you
So why are you afraid?

The Diamond In You

Most diamonds are formed within the Earth
through extensive pressure and heat
Being shaped and molded, to and fro
until they are complete

You are a precious diamond
an exceptional beauty, a gem
A special one of a kind
especially designed by and for him

The pressures of life come to tear you down
and try to deter you away
The enemy uses your fears against you
and try to lure you astray

The heat and pressure mixed together
can soon take its toll
But keep in mind during these times
that God is still in control

He promised never to leave you
even in the midst of the flames
Just trust in his plan for you
as you call on his name

For this too shall pass
for you are a diamond shining bright
Through your morning of adversities
and your hardships at night

You'll go through some trials in your life
and tribulations will come to
But only because God wants to shape and mold
and cultivate the diamond in you

Increase

No matter what's going on in your life right now
know that God is a God of increase and knows
what you go through
He is the God of multiplication, not subtraction
and he wants to increase you!

Trials and tribulations will come
and make you feel like you have a loss, some way diminished
They can appear as if you're on a decreased side of life
but God is a God who will replenish

Sometimes you do lose something
but that won't be the end of your story
Even if it seems as if things are being taken away,
don't be fooled
for God is and always will be the God of increase,
honor and glory

He's still in the multiplication business
He's working on an answer for you right now
From the land of loss to the land of increase
He knows how to get you there, to let you fall, he won't allow

The Lord shall increase you more & more, you and your children
the promise for you and your family is true
Increase, more and multiply
look at all what God will do for you

Because your heavenly father is a God of increase
He has a way of making your dreams come true
Greater than what you expected
even if seems as if things have been taken from you

So spend less time thinking about what you've lost
and focus on what he's going to bring
God is working all things together for your good
He knows exactly how to work out everything

Just trust and know that he is God
whose power and love will never cease
Who wants to bless you abundantly
and in your life, multiply and increase

Distractions

God said for us to set our focus
on things above and not the things below
That means we must concentrate on him
and all of our distractions, they must go

A distraction is anything that takes your focus
from what you're supposed to do
Distractions don't look like distractions
until they finish distracting you

Distractions are coming more frequently
trying to make our walk deferred
So it's time for us to center our attention
and totally focus on God's Word

The enemy uses these distractions to pull you
to lose your way, your will, and your fight
It is during our darkest moments
that we must focus more to see the light

Peter lost his focus on the water
because of the distraction of the boisterous wind
Just enough to lose a little faith
I'm pretty sure he did not intend

When life gets a little blurry, adjust your focus
distractions are going to come but stay on track
For you were created with a purpose
no need for unwanted setbacks

It's time to be habitually focused
Kingdom bound and spiritual impaction
Concentrate on our lives for God
Focus ahead...no distractions

Just Because

We need to give God all his praises
for all the things that He does
Not just a Sunday praise
but a praise...just because

Just because you woke us up this morning
Just because you brought us out
Just because you never left us
and guided us throughout

Just because you loved us first
and just because you made ways
We give you all the honor and glory
and we give you all the praise

Just because you gave your only son
and just because your love outpour
Just because we love you
knowing you love us even more

Just because of your grace and mercy
Just because you are Lord of Lords
The Alpha and Omega, the beginning and end
with you we can be restored

Just because you are God
the independent, the true, the one
We praise your holy name
the Father, the Spirit and the Son

In all that you have done
loving us in spite of our flaws
We praise and we worship you
our Heavenly Father...just because

That Thing

Everyone has a thing
no matter what it may be
That keeps you from moving forward
holding you in bondage, unfree

That thing that pricks your heart
and tries to destroy your mind
The enemy uses it to control you
and keep you spiritually confined

That thing can be your health,
your spouse, your children, your job
Your finances, your church
anything that the enemy can rob

It constantly picks away at you
making you pace the floor
With each passing day
you are more worried than before

But that's not God's intention
He does not want us to worry or be afraid
He freed us from all of that
when his sacrificial debt was paid

This thing that is taunting you
on this very day
In Jesus' name, I ask of you
to release yourself and give it away

Just trust and know you are more than a conqueror
through this thing, you can withstand
Give it all to him
just place it into his hands

Once in his hands, leave it
continue praising and worshipping
And watch him move on your behalf
for your good, he'll fix that thing

It's Deeper Than A Pill

Some turn to pills to get through tribulations
some to relax, less stress or just to sleep
But no pill can quite compare
to the ultimate peace that goes way down deep

Things change in a matter of minutes
you sometimes find yourself in a midst of a hurricane
The emotions swaying to and fro
as your tranquility and peace start to drain

If it's not one thing, it's another
the enemy comes to destroy your mind
He steals your joy, wrecks your soul
leaving you standing there naked and blind

There is a way to gain ultimate peace
which passes all understanding
Add with a little faith and a dash of trust
the peace that God provides is outstanding

Unlike a pill, it don't just abide within your system
but it goes deep to embed in your soul
It fills you up with harmony and freedom
an inner peace that makes you whole

Free up your mind and avoid bondage
praise and pray each and every day
You soon will start to discover
your anxieties and fears drifting away

Just like he rebuked the winds
and unto the sea he said, peace be still
And just like that, he can do it within you
give you the peace that goes deeper than a pill

Did You Listen?

One of the greatest benefits of Salvation
is to hear God speak to us one on one
For without personal communication
an intimate relationship...we have none

But some have a hard time hearing his voice
although to us, he constantly speaks
It is us who are not listening
making us spiritually weak

To know the voice of God, you must know him
If you don't, his voice you won't recognize
He speaks to us through the Holy Spirit
gently himself, to us, he applies

God will speak to the hearts
of those who prepare themselves to hear
He wants to talk with you
He is patiently waiting near

Lean not unto your own understanding
strive to be with him on one accord
I guarantee he will answer you
just expect to hear from the Lord

With expectation you will hear
the subtle voice of God within
If you are questioning did he speak,
you need to ask yourself...did you listen?

Reflection

A mirror is a reflective surface
that reflects a clear image of what it sees
No distortion or make believe
but the mere truth to all degrees

Everyone has a different reaction
when they catch their own reflection
Some dance and prance, get a little vain
some run out in the other direction

Some may not say anything
but you can see them trying to hide
Covering-up exposed parts of their being
embarrassed and cutting their eye to the side

Some turn their backs to the mirror
while some burst out in tears
Because it shows so much of themselves
the disappointments, imperfections and their fears

There's a lot to say about the person
in the mirror looking back at you
A story unfolded and partially untold
of all you went through

The mirror is a powerful tool
it can cause you to sob and weep
For it forces you to deal with yourself
on a level that is so deep

God created us into his own image
are with us, a divine connection
And if that's not what you see when you look into the mirror
then it's time to evaluate and fix your reflection

Act On What You Hear

Don't fool yourself into thinking you're a listener
when you are anything but
Letting the Word go in one ear and out the other
as your mind remains shut

One needs to act on what they hear
not just listening but doing too
Following the path
that God laid out for you

Those who hear but don't act
are like those who glance in the mirror but didn't catch a view
They have no idea what they look like
and forget within a minute or two

But whomever catches the revealed counsel of God
even a glimpse out of the corner of their eye
And sticks with it like glue
and in his life the Word, they apply

Will experience a life anew
so full of joy, life abundantly
No chains, no bondage
A life totally free

He promises to be with you, protect you
be your strength and for you provide
To love you, give you peace and answer you
and in Him you can hide

So when God speaks to you
listen with your heart not just your ear
Let his Word abide within you
and act on what you hear!

Are You Dressed?

It seems when we take one step forward,
we end up two steps back
Trials and tribulations sway us
and we tend to fall off track

The devil is always busy chasing,
trying to put his hooks in you
Just like God has a plan for your life,
unfortunately, the devil does too

It's time to dress to fight,
for the battle is not on land
But a spiritual warfare is in place
and your soul is at hand

So gird your waist with truth,
the body's strongest part
Wear the heart plate of righteousness,
for it covers and protects your heart

Cover your feet with peace,
a troublemaker is not what you are
You're more than a conqueror
and you prove that in this war

Carry the shield of faith,
it protects you from darts of the enemy
Don't forget who you belong to,
no more bondage, you have been set free

Wear the helmet of salvation
and carry the sword of the spirit, God's word
Because of your deliverance and redemption,
from head to toe shall be gird

Every day won't be easy
every day wont be the same
But the battle is already won
when you call on Jesus name

Keep your faith, stay strong,
God knows the fight you're in
He promised never to leave you
He'll be there until the end

This spiritual warfare is very real,
time should not be hee-hawed
You have to stand strong,
and wear the whole armor of God.

Because He Lives

Today is not about a bunny or eggs
but it's about three nails and a cross
It's not about a basket or a hunt
but about saving souls that were lost

It's about a redeemer
who sacrificed his life for you
It's about a savior
who wanted to create in you anew

It's about a love so pure
so unconditional…so deep
That he gave up his life
so our life, we may keep

It's about the blood that was shed
that carried our names with each drop
It's about a connection, a power
that will never stop

It's about the empty tomb
and the cloth on the floor
It's about the goodness
that he came to restore

We celebrate today
because 3 days ago, the sacrifice Jesus did give
And now we rejoice
because He lives!!

Do Not Stay.

David said "though I walk through the valley of the
shadow of death
He did not say "I Stay"
Nor set up camp, or build a house
or find somewhere for his head to lay

But in effect the valley is not your home
don't get discouraged, don't give in
Keep the faith and hold on tight
even though it appears to be bleak from where you have been

Although life will throw things against you
it will sometimes be hard, unfair and brittle
But cling on tight to your determined faith
and don't settle for the middle

You have to trust and you have to believe
God is the God of the middle not just the end
And even though you may not understand right now
on him, you need to lean and depend

Do not get stuck in the middle of your valley
keep moving forward, God's in control, he'll set you free
And this tribulation that you're going through
is just one more step toward your destiny

Though you may walk through the valley of the shadow of death
keep walking through as you pray..
Trusting and knowing God never left your side
rest if you must, but do not stay

I Am That I Am

I am the way, the truth and the light
no one comes to the father but through me
I am the gate, he shall be saved
shall go in and out, find pasture for I hold the key

I am the good shepherd
I lay my life down for my sheep
I am the resurrection and the life
He who believes in me, in death, his life he can keep

I am the bread of life
come to me and hunger no more
I am the light of the world
follow me, no darkness, just life light restore

My father is the vinedresser
I am the true vine
I want to bless you and keep you
make your life divine

I am The Rock, The Cornerstone
The Holy, The Lamb
I am The Alpha, The Omega
I am that I am

It Is Finished

Calvary is not just a place
but to think so, some do seem
It is where our savior saved us,
where our lives were redeemed

Because we were hostages
the ultimate price, Jesus paid
He gave his life as a ransom
and for us, to the father, a bridge was made

With every drop of blood was a name
for, he did not just die
But his blood was shed on Calvary
for the sins of you and I

You're cleansed by that blood
that loves, redeems, sanctifies and save
The precious blood that our savior
so graciously, to us, gave

Before he died, he prayed for us
knowing we would stumble and fall
Knowing all our faults, still loving us
on his holy name, we can call

See, Calvary isn't just a place
it's where Jesus hung, bled and died for me
It's where our debt was paid
no more bondage…we are set free

So my savior, the Great I Am
without a wrinkle, spot or blemish
Died on the cross at Calvary
for you and I…saying… "It is finished."

Paid In Full

For God so loved the world
that he gave his only begotten son
To save the world from sin
and get his work on earth done

Jesus left his throne
to be a living sacrifice
The sweetest debt I know
he paid the ultimate price

He came that we may have life
and have it abundantly
Saving us from ourselves
and setting our souls free

He humbled himself
and became just a man…
A man who was sent from heaven
saving his people throughout the land

He hung bled and died
up on calvary's cross
The greatest love of all
He counted up the cost

Jesus is The Way
He is The Truth and The Light
We need to honor and worship him
and praise him in sheer delight

The only begotten son
from our state, he did pull
Calvary's cross, because we were lost
our debt paid in full.

You Won't Be The Same

"When you put a seed into the ground, it doesn't grow into a plant unless it dies first." – 1ˢᵗ Corinthians 15:36, NLT

In order to live, you first have to die
to your plans, your emotions, your way and your will
Empty yourself completely
so that in you, God can fill

God has so many things
He wants to release to you today
But you have to get you
out of the way

Allow God to bury you
deep within him
So that you can spring forth with new life
filled up to the brim

People have thrown dirt on you
stepped on you, walked away
Thought you were going to die
knew you needed them, but still did not stay

But God is pulling you from the dirt
from the ground, He says to you LIVE
All that you'll ever need or ask for
in abundance, I will give

You were abused, misused
trampled upon the ground
But when you come up, you won't look the same
as you were when you went down

Heal the Boy

All grown up
from a boy into a man
You're going through so many changes
you just don't understand

So much anger from the years built up inside
yet you desire to want to run
Your mind is in a whirl, suffering silently
looking for a way out and can't find one

Trouble seems to follow
although for it…you do not seek
Your life's in quite a turmoil
and your future to you seems bleak

Doubts and fears try to take over
with each day it steals your joy
That's because although you grew
you didn't heal the boy

There is a man I know
who can heal, deliver and set free
Who can reach down deep into your soul, heal the boy
so you can be the man he wants you to be

He can strengthen you where you're weak
He can mend you back where you fell apart
If you just trust in him, Jesus, the great I Am
and believe with all your heart

He wants to create in you anew
He wants to make you whole
He wants to give you back
all the things the devil stole

Just let him in your heart
and he will come in and sup
Heal the boy, mend the man
He will clean you up

I stand here not just as your sister,
but a witness, because I know that this is true
Not only does he heal the boy,
but he heals little girls too.

Refusing To Be Ordinary

Refusing to be ordinary
is not an easy task
You must walk in boldness
with your head up high, wearing no mask

Refusing to be ordinary
means looking beyond what I can see
Delighting myself in God
seeing him manifest himself in me

Refusing to be ordinary
is being peculiar and standing out
Letting the beauty of myself
bubble over and stream about

Refusing to be ordinary
is standing strong even when I'm weak
Tears may flow on the outside
but my determination is at its peak

Refusing to be ordinary
a woman humble, meek, yet bold
Praying, searching, yearning
waiting for God's plan for her to unfold

Refusing to be ordinary
is what every woman's desire should be
Refusing to be ordinary
to change, to be delivered and set free.

That Something On The Inside

Is there something on the inside?
A burning, a kindling, ready to ignite?
Shut up in your bones,
A non-dimming light?

A something like fire
that makes you want to obey
That keeps you humble
and on your knees to pray

A something that keeps you going
and makes your flesh sit down
Tells self you get to die
you are more focused on the crown

Can you testify wanting to give up,
but that something wouldn't allow you to?
The push, the drive, the determination
knowing and trusting He will see you through

You can't be still
can't be quiet, you can't quit
That something won't let you give up
but beacons you to submit

Some of your good is at the bottom
Stir it up!! Taste and see that the Lord is good
Stir up the gift that's within you
and use it as you should

Something is on the inside
a burning, a kindling, a desire
Shut-up in your bones
ready to combust like fire

Let it use you
that something…you can't hide
Allow it to combust
that something on the inside

Turn On The Light

When you step into a room and its dark
and the gloom fills the room with fright
So that your vision is clear, what do you do?
Of course, you turn on the light!

For light stimulates sight
and makes things easier to see
Why would anyone want to be in darkness
and stumble and not be free?

Just like a dark room
the world can be a dark place
where you stumble and sometimes you fall
and there are times you feel displaced

Jesus said "as long as I am in the world,
I am the world's light"
There is no need to be in darkness for He is here
He will be there for your day and through your night

Whatever you are going through
God will not only bring you to it, but He will make you stronger
to be
Though you walk through the valley of darkness
He will be the light that you see

His Word is a lamp for your feet
and a light on the path for you
He is your beacon, your lighthouse, The Way
He will bring you through

You can rejoice even in your darkest place
and in Him, yourself delight
He will fill you up and keep you like only He can
but first, you must turn on the light

Unspeakable Joy

Are you just happy?
Just a feeling of an emotion?
Or does joy reside within
filled with love, honor and devotion?

Joy is something far great
a feeling beyond the soul
Produced by the Holy Spirit
one cannot contain or control

Having Joy will cause you to reflect
and have tears rolling down your face
Thinking how you came this far
nothing but His mercy and grace

Joy will have you praising and worshipping
because of the bubbling inside
Like fire shut-up within
that you can't shake nor hide

Joy will have you content
with peace that surpass all understanding
Although life seems to be distraught
and the world around you is demanding

Joy is from deep within
feeding you zest and zeal
And unlike happiness
joy, no one can steal

So if you're just happy today
God can offer you what no man can destroy
A peace of mind, a love unconditionally
an unspeakable joy!

Get In The Boat

Why are you drowning in tribulation and pain
and struggling to stay afloat
When God has all that you need
and he is telling you to just get in the boat

If you're trying to hide, believe me you can't
not behind title, job, church, bible or any place
He sees what you do, what you go through
He wants to bless you and help you about-face

He wants to abide in you and save you
for you are His…you belong to him
He wants to be a beacon in your life
for those times that may get dim

Just like the computer can convert
a file to a different format file
He wants to convert you
and change your lifestyle

If there is any doubt in your mind
where you need to start
Just confess the Lord Jesus with your mouth
and believe God raised him from the dead within your heart

We are here on this earth
to carry out His will
There is no need for us to worry
every need, He'll make sure is fulfilled

Just put your trust in God
put down them problems on your shoulder that you tote
Believe in my father to do what the bible says
and just…get in the boat

He Has His Hand Around My Towel

He has his hand around my towel
when I want to throw it in
Reminding me of who I am
and what I am within

He has his hands around my towel
when my hands want to go up
Filling me with his love
and overflowing my cup

He has his hands around my towel
when I want to sit and cry
A pity party is not for me
and He is the reason why

He has his hands around my towel
when I feel angry and depressed
Building me up inside
with his joy, peace and zest

He has his hands around my towel
and cradles me in his arm
Letting me know I am His
and to me will come no harm

He has his hands around my towel
and holds me when its dim
Reminding me every day
I'm more than a conqueror through him

I'm stronger than before
every day on his Word I'll stand
Trusting and knowing
my towel is in his hand

Meet Him At The Wall

Sometimes when life goes awry
we want to give up and all we do is cry
We seem to stumble and then we fall
but if only we just meet him at the wall

No one promised all good days
during the sunshine, there will be some haze
You find yourself in a spirally downfall
just come to him, meet him at the wall

At the wall, just one on one
just you alone with his holy son
To him, your cares are so small
take them to him, he will take care of it all

At the wall casting all your fears
that you have been harboring over the years
Releasing the anguish, hurt and all
standing there with him at the wall

At the wall you will find peace
your worries will be few, your faith increase
You will stumble, but now not fall
for you went to him at the wall

My God is loving with a listening ear
He's in control, there is nothing to fear
The pain, the hurt, the suffering…he knows it all
but he wants you to meet him at the wall

Present And Accounted For

Here I am Lord
present and accounted for
Willing to worship and praise you
now and forever more

There is so much to do
so much that I don't know
But I am a willing vessel
ready to learn and grow

Ready to serve
in God's army of love
Protected by his armor
and his angels from above

Changing my position
from "I can", to "I will"
Listening for your voice
and knowing when to be still

For when I am weak
I know that I am strong
Trough trials and tribulations
my heart still sings a song

I'm more than a conqueror
with this I will abide
When times get too rough
in you, I know I can hide

Serving is an honor
and a privilege to me
It represents a soul
is unbound and set free

So here I am, Lord
ready to join your corps
Muletta Hayes—
present and accounted for.

And His Name Shall Be Called Jesus

And His name shall be called Jesus
the name above all names
The Prince of Peace, The Lamb of God
The Son of Righteousness, to help put away your shames

The author and finisher of our faith, the root of David
The Word of God, the advocate, the way
He is the light, wonderful counsel
our debt, He selflessly did pay

Our chief cornerstone, King of Kings
The Messiah, The Truth, Our Morning Star
He promises never to leave you
and it doesn't matter where you are

Head of the Church, Lord of Lords
Our Redeemer, Lord of All
Resurrection of Life, Horn of Salvation
He answers when on Him we call

Call him in the morning,
Call him in the noon day or at night
He is the Holy one…He is the only one
who can make it right

He is Immanuel, the Christ
The Almighty, whose life for us he laid
The ultimate sacrifice for you and I
our sinful debt, He unselfishly paid

He is the Alpha and Omega, The Governor
every day he is the same
The Savior of this world of sin
and Jesus is his name.

When The Pain Is Too Much

When the pain is too much,
but yet instill you try
Floating slowly towards depression
and all you do is cry

When the pain is too much
and you're looking to console your heart
Trying to keep things together
as they seem to fall apart

When the pain is too much
holding on to your faith, you pray
Asking God for discernment
and to guide you along the way

When the pain is too much
and it feels like you're hanging by a limb
It's time to grab hold
and lean closer unto Him

When the pain is too much
and it's more than you can bare
Just trust in his word
for He will always be there

When the pain is too much
and it's hard to see down the road,
Remember his promises in his word
you don't have to bear the load

He told you to cast your burdens
for you to come to him, He will give you rest
He will hold your right hand and help you
for He cares and sends his best

Even unto your old age, He will carry you
he will carry you in his bosom and arm
Fear not, for he is with you
there is no need to be alarmed

When all seems lost
and you feel so out of touch
Just hold on to his everlasting hand
even when the pain is too much

Choose Ye This Day

There's a driving force in everyone's life
a force that no man can see
Whether it's God, the Holy Spirit
or the enemy with trickery

Everyone has a choice
to choose which one he feeds
The one that eats will grow
and in your life, it will lead

No man can serve two masters
the one you will love, the other hate
The choice is yours, free will
the choice to choose your fate

The Lord is coming like a thief in the night
we must be ready by what we say and do
He is coming when least expected
he prepared a place for me and you

In order to be ready, we must choose
whether to be ready or not
We must understand how frail we are
for some have seemed to forgot

No one knows the day or hour
no time for your mind to be to topsy-turve
The time has come to make a decision
choose ye this day whom you will serve

Are You Ready For Your New Name?

Our heavenly father is the God of Life
the one who can resurrect the dead
He is also the one who changes destinies
and abides within for us to be spirit-led

When God gives you a new name
it's to establish a new identity
The new name will represent the change
he has brought about in you and me

Jesus sees what you can be
regardless of where you are today
He knows what we are just the same
but loves us enough not to leave us that way

He changed Abram to Abraham, Sarai to Sarah
mother and father of many nations
Their descendants are even more numerous
than any of their expectations

He changed Jacob to Israel, having power with God
he struggled with God and overcame
He changed Simon to Cephus, Peter
He saw what he could be and The Rock he became

Destined for a new mission
your new name will reveal its divine plan
To assure you it will be fulfilled
just when he calls, say here I am

He will give you a white stone engraved with your newness
just for you and you alone to acclaim
A change, your purpose, your destiny…
Are you ready for your new name?

Renewed

The pressure of life weighing you down
the spirit of depression leading to solitude
Bruised and hurt and out of control
it's time to be RENEWED

Repentance is a new start
in turn is a new mind
We must confess our sins daily
to make ourselves become refined

It's time to regenerate, rejuvenate
restore, reinstate and mend
Re-establish, resume, repair
come back to, and start again

When your mind understands God's Word
it is gradually transformed by the Holy Spirit
When you feel it deep in your soul,
that's when you need to adhere it

We are all works in progress
there will be times when we stumble or fall upon our face
But God knows all about it
and will meet you in your dark place

He who began a good work in you
will perfect it until the day of Jesus Christ
Who gave his life unselfishly
the ultimate sacrifice

Although it may appear a little bleak
and your life seems to be misconstrued
I know a man who can change all that
redeemed, refresh, revived and renewed

Let Me Pray For You

Our Father, which art in heaven
hallowed be thy name
If these words aren't familiar to you
then your living may be in vain

Prayer is the telephone line
to talk to Jesus, you see
but if you are in doubt or cannot figure it out
then please allow me

Heavenly Father we come to you
as humbly as we know how
Acknowledging you are our savior
and seeking forgiveness now

Please come into our hearts
and create in us anew
Clean us up father as we know only you can
for we desire to be like you

Touch the sick and shut-in, Lord
and allow their healing to begin
Go in prisons and bless them, Father
be their comforter and their friend

Death is all around us
we know this to be true
We thank you Lord for waking us
we breathe today because of you

Please send a fresh anointing
let it envelop us as we walk through the door
So we will leave with an insight
we won't think like we did before

When our eyelids are shut
and we can praise you here no more
please welcome us into your kingdom
as you promised us before

We give you all the praise and glory
we worship you until the end
In Jesus' name it is that I pray
let us all say, Amen

Don't Look Back

Strong winds will blow, they may sway you
but don't allow them to get you off-track
Stay focused, keep it moving
and most important...don't look back

Within your life you've been in some storms
and along the way you've felt pain
But through it all, you've stood strong
with your head held high, you danced in the rain

Your heart was bruised but it recovered
and sometimes you were to blame
It's time to move forward and forgive yourself
and in it, find no shame

Don't spend all your time in the rearview mirror
it may make your situation seem worse
Your focus will be off-course
for you will end up in reverse

Life will always contain a challenge
emotional, physical and mentally you drain
But if you just hold out and keep your faith
God will definitely sustain

He promised you life full of abundance
and on his promise he will give
But if you don't let your past die
then your past will not let you live

Starting today, this is your Exodus
staying strong especially during an attack
Look up, look out, look forward,
but most importantly, don't look back!

The Struggle Is Real

The struggle is real, but it's necessary
to push you where you need to be
What is trying to kill you is part of God's plan
to drive you to your destiny

It's not the circumstances that's important
it's about how you handle it
Holding tight to your undying faith
there is no option to quit

Some of your greatest victories
come from your hardest fights
Trust in God in the midst of your storm
especially during your weeping nights

Knowing he was in your beginning
before your beginning began
And at your ending before you get there
for your life, he has a plan

For you are on the forefront of his mind
you, God is willing to chase
He wants your genuine worship from your heart
and his spirit for you to embrace

Worship him in spirit and in truth
with your whole soul and mind
He desires you to be closer to him
making himself easy to find

In your times of trials and tribulations
be strong, steadfast, encouraged and still
Cling closer through praise and worship
because although necessary, the struggle is real.

In Conclusion...

It took some time for me to find God. All throughout my life I had heard of Him, but never had a relationship with Him. I did not know Him, but I am so glad that He knew me. He has blessed me with the gift of poetry and I want to share it with everyone. If I could just help one person find that special relationship, it would please my heart; for God is not a religion, He is a relationship. We all need love and guidance and I pray that my poems help to spread and accomplish that task. Some people may never see the inside of a church to get the Word. I would like to try to be a link to help them at least desire to abide with Him.

Sometimes God puts us in the dark to show us He is the light. I wrote these poems to let people know that we fall down and we make mistakes, but God is our helping hand and will help us get back up again. We have a forgiving God, a loving God! Prayerfully, my poems will inspire relationships and connections to our father like no other. When you put God first, everything falls into place. My book of Inspirational Poetry was written…to prick your heart, convict your soul and renew your mind.

CPSIA information can be obtained
at www.ICGtesting.com
Printed in the USA
LVHW022155150920
666084LV00003B/623